ALPHA

FOR MY PAPA

First U.S. edition 2015

Library of Congress Catalog Card Number 2014951397
ISBN 978-0-7636-7852-4

20 19 18 17 16 15
TLF 10 9 8 7 6 5 4 3 2 1

Printed in Dongguan, Guangdong, China

The illustrations were done in watercolor, gouache, pencil, and colored pencil.

Candlewick Press
99 Dover Street
Somerville, Massachusetts 02144

visit us at www.candlewick.com

ALPHA

ISABELLE ARSENAULT

CANDLEWICK PRESS

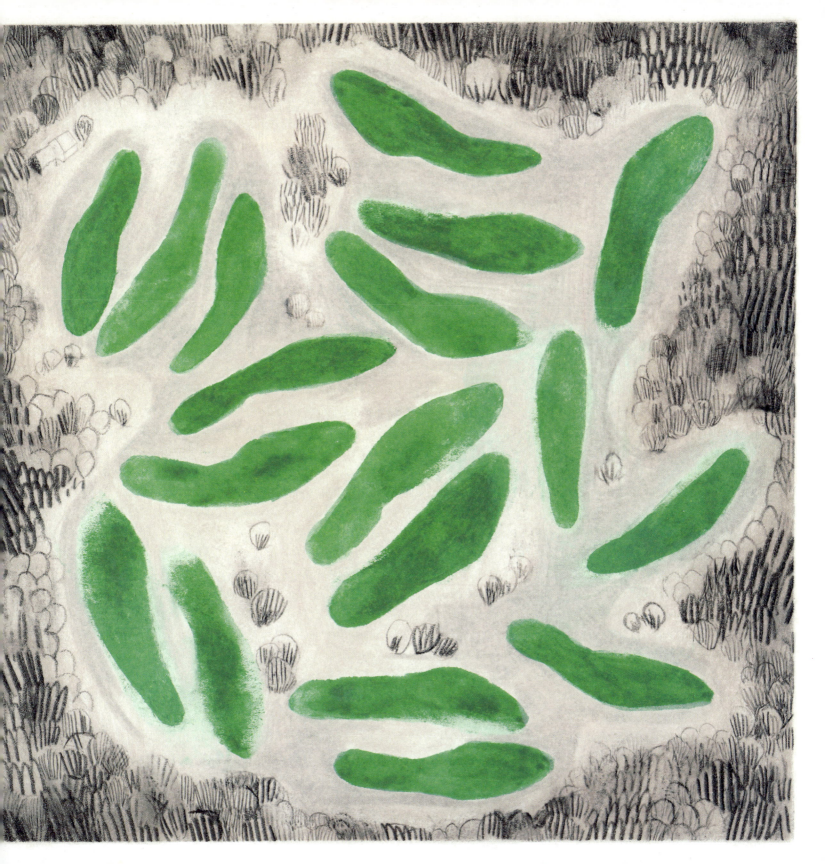

NOVEMBER

OSCAR

PAPA

SIERRA

TANGO

VICTOR

X-RAY

The NATO phonetic alphabet, or more accurately, the International Radiotelephony Spelling Alphabet, is used by various emergency services, including firefighters, police, the military, and the Red Cross, as a way to communicate clearly and precisely in urgent situations. When sending a message, each letter in the word is spelled out using this alphabet. For example, *cat* would be "Charlie-Alpha-Tango." NATO adopted a standardized version of this alphabet in 1956 and has used it ever since. In some versions, *Alpha* appears as *Alfa* and *Juliet* becomes *Juliett*.

In addition to being a helpful way to learn the alphabet, this abecedarian offers the reader a way of communicating in an internationally recognized code. Each page, each letter, each word, and each image invite investigation, increase vocabulary, and offer the reader an opportunity to reflect on the many possible interpretations each letter holds.